MW01033514

The River of Wisdom

Reflections on Yoga, Meditation, and Mindful Living

Darren Main

Author of *Yoga and the Path of the Urban Mystic*

©2015 The River of Wisdom
Reflections on Yoga, Meditation and Mindful Living by Darren Main

ISBN-13: 978-1517004552
ISBN-10 1517004551

Printed and bound in the United States of America

Cover, Design, Print & Epub Production by Michael Fantasia

Surya Rising Books
PO Box 14584
San Francisco, California 94114

For my son Jaden

From the first time I held you I realized that everythingup to that point—the joy, the pain, the spiritual practice, was all to prepare me for being a daddy. You are by far the very best part of my extraordinary life.

Endorsements

In River of Wisdom, Darren offers precious insights and inspirations, beautiful stepping stones into the eternal, divine, ceaseless and boundless River of Life. Each passage is, itself, both a reflection of the river which flows through us all and also a pathway into the river, pulling us into the sacred waters, out of the dry maya in which we live on the shore.

> —Sadhvi Bhagawati Saraswati
> President, Divine Shakti Foundation
> Secretary-General, Global Interfaith WASH Alliance
> Director, International Yoga Festival
> Parmarth Niketan Ashram, Rishikesh, India

The River of Wisdom is the perfect title for Darren Main's newest contribution to the yoga and healing arts literature. Using utterly simple language, Main clearly conveys the essential elements of yoga and mindful living in ways that make them accessible and practical for anyone interested in deeper self understanding, self-acceptance, and self-transformation. These 108 insightful statements reflect the mindful experience of a dedicated yogi on the path of making life better. Main gets the plurality of yoga paths and philosophies, weaving and sharing in original ways that no less bring forward ancient kernels of yogic wisdom This is a book that yoga students and teachers, contemplative practitioners, and anyone on a healing path will read over and over again.

> —Mark Stephens
> Yoga Teacher and Author

Darren has another book that brings the distillation of the teachings of yoga into a practical understanding adaptable to anyone regardless of religious or cultural background. His mastery of expression, humor and insight show how deeply spiritual teachings have embedded themselves in his life and sadhana. In turn he is able to translate them into transformative experiences for others.

—Yogi Amrit Desai
Author of *Amrit Yoga*

Drawing on the author's many years of experience in yoga and meditation, River of Wisdom gives us, through delicious and poetic prose, an opportunity to sensually experience the peaceful beauty of every moment. No matter where you are or what you are doing, stop, sit, read or contemplate a page and cultivate gratitude for all you have.

—Beryl Bender Birch
Director, The Hard & The Soft Yoga Institute, Co-founder of The Give Back Yoga Foundation & author, *Power Yoga and Yoga for Warriors* and Director/ Co-founder of The Give Back Yoga Foundation

Darren Main has long been my go to guy for yoga inspiration. In this collection, he continues to give us his wisdom as a lifelong yogi. Each passage can be its own theme for a yoga class or a fitting daily meditation. Bravo. Please get this book and have a taste of Darren's experience and knowledge.

—Darren Littlejohn
Yoga Teacher and author of *The 12-Step Buddhist*

Darren's created a playful compilation of 108 thoughtful reflections. A true gift for any yogi or aspiring yogi hoping to live with intention.

—Kimberly Wilson
Founder of Tranquil Space

Darren Main draws from his rich experience as a yoga instructor and mindfulness practitioner, delivering thought-provoking gems in this accessible and inspirational collection.

—Ashley Simpson Shires, *SF Yoga Magazine*

Whether a few words or several each quote can be savored like a koan; the meaning of each word made more important by its combination with the others. Nothing unnecessary. Greedily I say: I wanted more.

—Kyczy Hawk
Founder of SOAR™, author of *Yoga and The Twelve Step Path* and *Life in Bite Sized Morsels* www.yogarecovery.com

Darren does it again with his heart wisdom. I like to start my busy days with a simple reading that I can reflect upon throughout the day to lean on for support and be a reminder to guide me back home to my heart and soul. How lucky we are to receive these simple yet profound reminders, come home. Thanks Darren.

—Les Leventhal,
YogaWithLes
Author of *Two Lifestyles, One Lifetime*

In his new book Darren Main has taken his lifelong experience on the spiritual path and has distilled it into 108 modern day yoga sutras. Each one of Darren's sutras contains layers of wisdom that unfold more and more deeply with each reading. This book will benefit everyone in the yoga and spiritual community.

—Gary Kissiah
Yoga teacher, lawyer and author of *The Yoga Sutras of Patanjali-Illuminations Through Image, Commentary and Design*

A yoga practice offers you so much more than just stretching and posing. Darren generously shares the divine insights of his own practice, inviting you to a more profound experience of yoga and self inquiry. A gift to read!

—Amy Ippoliti, yoga teacher, author, and co-founder of *90 Monkeys*

A beautiful, thoughtful collection of insights to help focus any yoga practice, on or off the mat. I recommend it.

—Iosha Silver
author of *Outrageous Openness: Letting the Divine Take the Lead* and *Change Me Prayers: The Hidden Power of Spiritual Surrender*

Potent and gentle, pliable and strong, timely and timeless, artful and practical, earnest and approachable... my new meditation companion... eminently touching and inspired... may rivers of this wisdom continue feeding seas of compassion for years to come!

—Sam Jackson,
Crystal Bowl Meditations, VibrantStillness.com

Darren Main strikes again with substantive testament to the richness of his practice, here with an intimacy that can speak to everyone.

—Jason Bowman
Writer and Yoga Teacher

Darren's every word speak directly to my heart. His insights capture the revelations I have experienced through my own meditation practice and through many years of living and serving the underprivileged community in Rishikesh India—the homeland of yoga and meditation. The River of Wisdom is a lifetime of spiritual reflection distilled to its essence. It is a book everyone should have on their coffee table.

—Shahla Ettefagh
President & Founder of Mother Miracle Community Program
India Rishikesh www.mothermiracle.com

I was moved by each and every page that I read, inspired to face my day and face my life with renewed energy and a fresh commitment to mindfulness."

—Brian Leaf
author of *Misadventures of a Garden State Yogi*

Darren Main has figured out how to stream divine wisdom and luckily he has decided to share it with the world. River of Wisdom is chock full of nuggets of enlightenment. Each page is a new lesson, some are 'tweetable,' while others fill the page with inspiration. Use this book to inspire your life, your yoga classes, and your meditations.

—Elise Marie Collins
Author of *Chakra Tonics* and *An A-Z Guide to Healing Foods*

Introduction

I sat with tears in my eyes, looking out over the Ganges River as it flowed from the Himalayas. I wondered how many holy men and women had sat in that very spot over the course of thousands of years—all of them in deep prayer and meditation.

I am no stranger to tears, having faced so many demons through my Twelve-Step work, but this was different, very different.

Even now, I could not tell you why I was crying. But I can say with absolute certainty, they weren't tears of sorrow. They were more like rivers of joy, pouring from my eyes and down my cheeks, mirroring the river before me.

Something much bigger than me inspired this joy, and that profound joy left clarity and vision in its wake. During my first trip to India, my morning practice revealed something beautiful beyond words to me. And yet, being human, I tried to use words anyway.

Since then I have experienced similar moments. They pass through the busyness of my life, but always seem to leave nuggets of wisdom behind. They have helped to mold and shape my view of the world. Though I often get swept away in the seemingly endless to-do list of my life, my perception of the world, of myself, and of my relationships with others, has slowly, over time, healed and transformed into something dramatically new and different.

Meditations often feel dreamlike — certainly leaving the mind more illuminated — but they often lack tangible revelations on which to fall back in times of struggle. So over the years, I have kept journals and notepads nearby to jot down thoughts and observations immediately following my practice.

I have come to believe that a river of wisdom flows through each of us. Yet drinking from this river requires the non-judgemental witnessing that only spiritual practices like prayer, yoga, and meditation can provide. This book is the result of my own practice.

Some of my reflections are colored with deep emotion, others with moments of clarity. Some reflections are a bit silly; others quite practical.

You may find some of my insights helpful; others you may dismiss entirely. Some passages may touch something true and authentic within you, while others may strike you as complete hogwash. You may read this book from cover to cover, or open to a random page to see what jumps out. Perhaps you want to reflect on a passage before you sit in meditation, or maybe this book will keep you company as you sit in the loo.

I can only be certain that there is no right and no wrong—not in spiritual practice, and certainly not in these pages. How you choose to use this book is up to you.

My only hope is that these thoughts and reflections, composed over many years, will inspire you to keep your commitment to your own spiritual practice strong. May you go deeply within yourself to find your own truth and drink from the river of wisdom that flows through you.

Namaste,

Darren Main

www.darrenmain.com

The River of Wisdom

1

Silence—true silence is universal. It is the
profound stillness at the center of everything—
at the center of every relationship—at the
center of yourself. While it is always there, it
can only be experienced beyond the veil of
judgment, expectation, and attachment. From
time to time, a person can spontaneously
enter into a perfect moment of silence
when dancing, watching a sunset, holding
an infant, or making love; but for most,true
silence remains elusive at best. Yet through
various forms of meditation and prayer this
veil can be lifted, allowing that inner silence
to wash through you, leaving in its wake a
cleansed mind and a compassionate heart.

2

Mindfulness is the bedrock of all spiritual
practice. With mindfulness, the simple
becomes profound, and the common
becomes extraordinary. Without mindfulness,
even gold and silver will quickly lose their luster.

3

All great myths and stories follow a similar
pattern. The hero gets distracted and questions
his power. He struggles and flounders until
he is able to face his perceived weakness.
Ironically, it is the struggle that makes him
stronger and enables him to meet his destiny.
Without the struggle, without missing the mark,
without getting lost in the mire of the journey,
growth would not be possible. We tend to
think of life's struggles as the cause of our
suffering, when in fact, struggle reveals our
true power and unlocks our latent potential.

4

Gratitude is both a vaccine and an antidote for grief. Grief may be an inevitable fact of life, but gratitude has the power to transform the experience of grief from agonizing suffering to profound joy.

5

Meditation is the alchemist of the soul.

It transforms disappointment into acceptance;

betrayal into forgiveness;

scarcity into abundance;

loneliness into self acceptance;

fear into love;

despair into hope;

anxiety into peace;

and apathy into compassion.

Sculpting the future and healing the
past can only happen through mindful
action in the present moment.

7

So many people confuse attachment with love. Attachment to someone implies control; loving someone assumes unconditional acceptance. Attachment leads to grief and loneliness when the person is no longer near—or even sometimes when he or she is in the very same room. Love is the realization that there is no distance between you and the other—whether they are across the room, around the world, or beyond the veil of death.

8

True power—not to be confused with
worldly power—is found at that beautiful
and sacred spot where will and surrender
merge into an unstoppable force.

9

The law of karma is like the wind—blowing
on all. Whether you are good or evil, bright or
dim, kind or unkind, there is no escaping the
effects of your thoughts and the actions that
arise from those thoughts. In fact, the only
difference between the wise and the ignorant
is that an illuminated mind erects windmills
while the ignorant mind builds weather vanes.

10

Why do we call yoga a practice?
The yoga poses of life—the grief, the fear,
the uncertainty—rarely offer us the option
of coming to child pose or modifying the
posture. The yoga mat offers us a safe
and controlled environment in which we
can witness our challenges, embrace
our discomfort, and hold space for our
struggles. A yoga practice doesn't prevent
the storms of life, but it does teach us to
weather those storms more gracefully.

11

The windmill doesn't try to control the wind
or demand that it blow in another direction.
It simply surrenders to the wind, and in so
doing becomes a source of immense power.
The water wheel doesn't attempt to change
the course of the river; it simply surrenders to
the flow and allows the power of the river to
be expressed through it. Most see surrender
as a form of weakness, when in reality,
surrender is the source of all true power.

12

The hardest part of any yoga practice
is rolling out your mat.

13

Apathy is the bushel basket under which the ego hides its fear of being powerless. It is easier to become apathetic when there are no words or actions sufficient to comfort a wounded body, a grieving heart, or a shattered community. And so we look away and avoid awkward conversations under the guise that we don't want to upset others. Yet, the most powerful posture for a healer to take is that of the witness. To stand and witness a person or community devastated by suffering, and to let them know that while they suffer they have a hand to hold, offers the most potent medicine of all—compassion.

14

When infused with compassion, even the most useless snake oils have the power to heal broken hearts and shattered souls.

15

In most forms of exercise one's breath follows
the movement — the faster and harder you
work, the faster and harder you will breathe.
In yoga, the exact opposite is true. Rather
than changing the breath to match one's
movement, movement is changed to follow
the breath. In doing so, a yogi gains immediate
and unconditional access to the deepest
levels of consciousness, because just as
breath and movement are connected, so
too is the breath bound tightly to the mind.

16

The narrow edge between comfort
and discomfort is to a yogi what a
grain of sand is to an oyster.

17

People slip spontaneously into moments of concentration all the time—while reading a book, exercising, playing chess, or creating art. A yogi seeks to experience that same level of concentration intentionally in a practice known as dharana—the act of purposefully narrowing the mind's focus on the breath, the sensations of the body, a mantra, or a prayer bead. This consistent and purposeful focusing of the mind while on the yoga mat or meditation cushion gives the yogi the same level of focus in life, allowing for wild creativity and unfathomable productivity.

18

The great paradox of life is that to fully live,
we must let a piece of ourselves die.

19

Although you could open a can of soup with a hammer, a stone, or even your teeth if you didn't mind making a mess or chipping a tooth, a much wiser approach would be to use a can opener. The breath is like a can opener for the soul. Can you explore the depths of your being without conscious breathing? Sure. The more relevant question is, why would you want to?

20

Non-attachment doesn't mean you forgo possessions, pleasure, or comfort. It simply means you are at peace when those things fail to show up in your life. It means that while you can enjoy moments of ease, you are equally at peace when pain, hardship, and struggle define a given moment.

21

Instead of asking, "How can I ease my suffering?" yoga would have us ask, "How can I better serve my brothers and sisters?" Because only in answering the latter can we hope to answer the former.

22

What I can tell you is that yoga is about removing the muck by shining the light of awareness on it. That is why yoga is so hard. None of us wants to look at the muck, but looking at it is the only way to dissolve it. Thus, there are many times that a yogi may feel filled with darkness. It's not that the darkness arrived because of yoga; it's that yoga made you aware of all the things that were holding you back. The good news is that with this awareness, you have the opportunity to dissolve the muck once and for all. However great the doubt, however deep the despair, you can take comfort in knowing that you are feeling these things because your yoga is doing exactly what it was designed to do. You can also take refuge in the knowledge that whatever you are feeling—whether high or low—will pass, because it always does.

23

Standing at the end of a diving board looking at the water never made the water warmer, but it will make taking the plunge unnecessarily hard.

24

What is it to succeed in yoga?

Success in yoga means finding the
smile buried deep beneath the pain
and discomfort of any moment.

Success in yoga is knowing that others
were able to find a smile beneath their pain
and discomfort because you were near.

Success in yoga is speaking to
yourself and others with compassion
and kindness, even when you want
to wield your words as weapons.

Success in yoga is to listen
more than you speak.

Success in yoga is when mindfulness
celebrates the joyful moments and
becomes a refuge for the painful ones.

Success in yoga is to be grateful even for
your pain, suffering, and challenges.

Success in yoga is willingly taking the time to
put the needs of another ahead of your own.

Success in yoga is feeling fear rattle your
bones and then doing it anyway.

Success in yoga is not only finding your
purpose in life, but also finding the courage
and passion to live that purpose.

Success in yoga is remembering that it was
never about the number of times you fell but
rather the number of times you got back up.

25

Once we understand cause and effect, we can stop complaining about the effects of our choices. We can start making more mindful decisions about the thoughts we entertain, the actions we perform, the people with whom we associate, and the quality of life we want to live.

26

The mind is the only level at which any lasting
change can occur—it is the soil in which
we plant our hopes and fears, habits, and
patterns. What we plant in the mind will grow
and bear fruit. Just as it would be pointless
to complain about a carrot seed failing to
produce a tomato, it is equally pointless to
look at the garden of your life and complain
about what you see growing there. We
have to be willing to plant different seeds.

27

Just as a hug is the only way to express
yourself when words are inadequate,mudras,
or gestures, convey profound spiritual
experiences that cannot adequately
be expressed verbally. The most
powerful,universal and healing mudra is a
smile. When we overflow with joy, we cannot
help but smile spontaneously. And when
we are mired in doubt, fear, anxiety, and
depression, a smile creates a map in the
mind that leads us home to that joy that is
hidden in even the darkest moments of our
life. It is one thing to know that joy is possible
in any moment—in any situation. It is another
skill entirely to know when to find that joy
when your world is crumbling around you.
The map is with you always—just smile!

28

Guilt is like tarnish on a piece of silver. It
effectively obscures beauty and radiance,
but can never lessen its true value. Just as
the true beauty and value of silver is revealed
with a little bit of polish, your true worth
will shine with regular spiritual practice.

29

Most people spend years trying to feng shui their lives—to decorate and reorganize life in such a way that order and peace will finally arrive. One can decorate and redecorate for years, but a fresh coat of paint is not going to patch the cracks in your foundation—the only way to do this is through the practice of non-attachment.

30

The truth about yourself is so near, so close,
that it is very difficult to perceive. Just as it is
difficult to style your hair, apply makeup, or
shave without a mirror, we require a mirror
of sorts to spiritually groom ourselves. For
most, that mirror is relationships with others.
People who wear masks of untrustworthiness,
dishonesty, selfishness, and greed see
those qualities reflected back from everyone
they meet—even the most noble souls who
cross their paths. But people who have put
their masks aside are able to experience
compassion, love, and wholeness in
others, even in their adversaries—even in
those who are still mired in a tangled web
of fear, insecurity, and abrasiveness.

31

Yoga and meditation help us to achieve physical health, emotional balance, more connected relationships, and a more satisfying life. But to measure spiritual practice by these benefits is to miss the point entirely. The true measure of our practice is how we respond to life when we fall short of these things— when the body falls ill or the heart breaks.

32

Evolution is messy. Oftentimes our brains
evolve more quickly than our capacity to love.
Science has unlocked many mysteries of the
universe by harnessing the human capacity
for critical thinking, logic, and observation. But
without a spiritual science to help the heart
keep pace, disaster is often the outcome.
Rather than clean sources of energy, we
develop atomic bombs. Rather than medicines
that heal we develop biological and chemical
weapons. Rather than technologies that allow
us to share ideas and communicate, we
find ourselves more isolated and lonely than
ever. Yoga, meditation, and other mystical
practices are the spiritual counterpoint to
western science. One unlocks the mind,
the other opens the heart; and together
they reveal humanity's true potential.

33

We live in a world that asks us to do rather than be; to achieve rather than shine; to form relationships that fulfill needs rather than celebrating wholeness. When we stop that cycle by practicing mindfulness, the axis on which the world spins shifts entirely, and nothing you knew before will be of any value.

34

The world would have us fill every space and occupy every corner of the mind. Yoga asks us to become empty; to come to the practice in openness and to allow the practice to remove our notions of good and bad,rich and poor, health and disease; to sit and simply witness without shame, without guilt, and without judgment. Yoga allows us to let go of everything and hold on to nothing. It allows us to let go of our preconceptions about who or what God is, what it means to live a spiritual life, and how to achieve enlightenment. Whether slowly or in an instant, yoga empties us. What remains is a silence that surpasses understanding,is beyond words, and gives us the eyes to witness the suffering of the world, the ears to hear the world calling out for compassion, and the heart to answer that call.

35

It is easy to make the mistake of thinking yoga is about touching your toes when in fact yoga is about learning to touch others. Likewise, many people think the purpose of meditation is a perfectly still mind, when in fact, it is a more compassionate heart. Spiritual practice is measured by one's ability to ease the suffering of the world one breath at a time.

36

Many look at the blessings in their lives—
money, talent, love, abundance, and so
on—and say, "I must be one of the chosen
ones."But the blessings in your life were
not bestowed upon you to help you live
a life of ease, but rather a life of service.
You were chosen—chosen to serve.

37

A teacher's job is to see students' potential before they can see it themselves; teachers need to have the faith and foresight to know they can actualize that potential and the wisdom to help students chart their course. It is only with this inner knowing that a teacher can invite the student, over and over again, to the edge of their comfort—and then give them a gentle nudge. In effect, a teacher is like the mother bird who can see her chicks flying before they realize they have wings.

38

Within your ego mind there is a prison cell. Its bars are made of resentment and the door is hung on the hinges of disappointment and unfulfilled expectations. It is a cell, or so you imagine, for those you have not yet forgiven. This prison cell only lacks one thing—a lock for the door. And so you must hold the door shut by force of will— expending tremendous energy to hold the door shut— energy that would otherwise be used to cultivate joy, creativity, and passion.

Many believe bliss and gratification to be
synonyms, when in fact they are antonyms.
Bliss is the nature of your most true Self
and it is with you anytime you become still
enough to listen. Gratification is what you
seek to fill the imagined emptiness, and
is generated by a false sense of self.

40

Attachment is the act of trying to control, manipulate, or sculpt the outside world in such a way that we lose sight of our true nature. Nonjudgmental observation allows a yogi to experience the external world as a mirror reflecting back one's true nature.

41

As a child, my father was a god to me—at
times I loved him, at times I feared him,
but I always wanted to be like him. As an
adolescent, I resented my father for the sin
of being human—for not being the god of
my childhood. Then, as a young man, I felt
sorry for my father because, in my arrogance,
I believed he knew nothing and I knew
everything. It was not until I held my own
son for the first time that I truly understood
my father. Now I can appreciate the man he
is and the man he helped me to become.

42

When we practice a yoga posture designed
to challenge our balance, the use of a gazing
point or drishti is a most effective way to
maintain physical equanimity. The act of
gazing without judgment or attachment is
easily the most effective way to bring stability
and balance to the pose. Likewise, when
the poses of life rob us of our equanimity,
gazing at the situation without attachment—
without judgment—is the most effective tool
we have to restore the mind to harmony.

43

Meditation alone cannot heal the world, but it can and does speed up the healing process.

44

The practice of meditation helps us to
organize our thoughts and structure our
ideas. Through the practice of meditation, we
can open to the creative flow that is waiting
to pour through us, infusing inspiration with
passion. Meditation puts the mind in order
and brings it under control, opening the door
to receive this free flow of perfect energy.

The unfocused mind is like a sledgehammer.
The focused mind is like a sharp axe.
Both tools can be used to take down
a tree, but the axe is going to be much
more efficient. Moreover, using the axe
will allow you to work more swiftly, thereby
saving much energy to get more done.

45

Jesus wisely counseled his followers to
search for the kingdom of heaven within
themselves; but to go within, one needs
a door, a key, and the courage to turn the
knob. Spiritual practice gives you all three.

46

It may seem humble to belittle yourself, but it is every bit as arrogant as grandiosity. Just as it is impossible to be more than you were created to be, it is also impossible to be less. When we pretend to be more or less, we are destined to search for wholeness everywhere except where it actually resides—within.

47

Typically, awareness is only directed to the pronounced sensations of the body—the pleasurable and the painful. In yoga, over and over again, we witness the sensations of the body—the pleasant and unpleasant; the subtle and the overwhelming—neither seeking nor avoiding, and regarding all equally and without prejudice. It is through this nonjudgmental observation of sensation that the wisdom of the body is received, true healing is achieved, and the door to the unconscious mind is cast open.

48

Like the tightly closed eyelids of a child trying
to escape the reprimand of a parent, there is
a part of the mind that needs to shut down
in the face of an internal dialogue that is
steeped in guilt, shame, and self-loathing.

49

Fundamentalism wears many masks, but always claims a monopoly on the Truth. Many people buy into fundamentalism in much the same way people buy cola to quench their thirst. There are elements of truth in fundamentalist thinking, just as water is an ingredient in cola. But just as the water loses much of its value when artificial flavors and colors are added, Truth loses its value when guilt, shame, and rigid dogma are present. Fundamentalism is to the soul what artificial sweetener is to the body.

50

Most people believe that pain and suffering are synonymous—that one begets the other. A yogi recognizes that pain is an unavoidable aspect of life and that suffering is a choice. Pain is what happens when you stub your toe, suffering is what your mind does with the sensation.

51

While religions and mystical traditions attempt to address the same spiritual questions with which all human beings wrestle, a religious person demands answers to questions that have no answers and attempts to demand harmony from the paradox of life. The result is less wisdom and varying degrees of both internal and external chaos. A mystic, on the other hand, contemplates and makes peace with unanswered questions. The great paradox is that sitting quietly with unanswered questions is the doorway to wisdom, balance, and peace.

52

It has been said that the body is the temple
of the spirit and the mind is the altar within
that temple. When we practice hatha yoga we
allow ourselves to come fully into the temple
of the body—not simply as a tourist wishing to
admire the fine architecture, but as a seeker on
a pilgrimage of deep devotion and reverence.

Meditation is the devotional practice of
placing on the altar of the mind that which
is sacred, holy, and revered. Just as you
would not place garbage on the altar of a
great temple, meditation allows a yogi to
place on the altar of her mind that which is
noble, pure, and free from attachment.

53

Do numbers hold spiritual significance?
Perhaps they do. For me, the most powerful
numbers are two and six because when you
multiply those numbers, you get the exact
amount of square feet required to roll out a
yoga mat. Even after years of practice, I'm
continually astounded that all I really need
to heal my body, open my heart, and still
my chaotic mind is twelve square feet.

54

The great spiritual tension between
the contemplative life of the monk and
spiritual activism in the world dissolves
entirely with one word—namaste: the
light in me bows to the light in you.

When meditation reveals the light in
ourselves, we naturally want to bow to
the light in all beings—to act on their
behalf in reverence and devotion.

When we truly see the light in another being,
our own light shines forth, dissolving the
seemingly eternal ache in our hearts and the
near constant struggle of the ego mind. To see
the light in one being—your own light or that
of another—is to win the cosmic game of hide
and seek and ease the suffering of the world.

55

Just as the light bulb allows the electricity
within it the opportunity to express its power,
the body allows prana—life energy—to
express itself. In yoga, our goal is to slowly
increase the wattage of the subtle body,
allowing prana to flow within us and through
us, leaving health and balance in its wake.

56

On a physical level, water is often called
the universal solvent because of its ability
to dissolve almost anything at the molecular
level. On a spiritual level it is the breath
which acts as a universal solvent, because
there is no trauma so great, no wound so
deep, no delusion so convincing, that deep
and mindful breathing will not dissolve it.

57

A Kula or spiritual community is like a nudist
camp for the soul. Not only are we given
the permission to remove our robes of
guilt, our suits of shame, and our masks
of false identity—we are encouraged to do
so. To become naked and hold nothing
back is to become truly beautiful.

58

To the unaware person, karma is the prison
in which the mind is held hostage. Because
of karma, an unaware person is doomed to
repeat the past in perpetuity as the seeds
planted yesterday bear bitter fruit tomorrow.
But to the mindful person, karma offers the
promise of freedom. Mindfulness allows us
to change our mind in the present, planting
new seeds that will bear sweet fruit.

59

True spiritual virtues can have no opposite,
but they can wear masks and costumes.

Joy often masquerades as anger;
innocence often dresses up as guilt; love
pretends to be fear. At the end of the
day, we discover that we don't need to
be fearful of these internal monsters—
we simply need to unmask them.

60

Forcing Your body into a yoga pose is like
brushing your teeth with a wire brush. You
may get rid of the plaque but gingivitis
will be the least of your concerns.

61

Resolutions, like all spiritual virtues, can be misused by the ego when mindfulness is absent. There are few things that will keep you in the bondage of habit like a grand resolution. It is like an empty box wrapped in the best of intentions, yet lacking anything of substance.

62

Yoga happens in the last 1% of a pose.

63

There is a need somewhere in this world
that only your dharma, fully expressed,
can fulfill. The reason there is such
overwhelming need in this world is because
an overwhelming number of people have
yet to find and express their dharma.

64

Hell is indeed a fiery pit—but it's not found in death, but rather in your stomach when you fail to speak your truth, live with integrity,or allow compassion to guide you.

65

To a yogi, the breath is the anchor that keeps the mind in the eternal now. Just as an anchored boat still shifts with the wind and moves with the current, so too will the mind continue to be affected by things beyond its control. Like the anchored boat, the mind will never drift too far from its mooring once it is anchored in the breath.

A closet is not a prison cell. There are no
bars on the windows, locks on the doors,
or shackles binding your feet. The closet
door is as easy to open as turning the knob.
To turn that knob requires the courage to
empty your hands of guilt, shame, and self-
loathing. Once you find that courage,you will
wonder why you waited so long to do it.

67

Can an atheist practice yoga? Can an agnostic
sit in meditation? Absolutely! Belief in God
is not a requirement for practice. The only
requirement for practice is the willingness to
accept that you are not God. To surrender to
the possibility that while an all-knowing God
may not govern the universe, neither do you.

68

A bird doesn't attempt to swim, and a
cat doesn't attempt to fly. Yet both are
completely content. Their dharma is anchored
in instinct. Humans are continually trying
to live out of accord with their dharma
and so contentment remains elusive.

Yoga practice is the most natural thing in the world. The body was designed to move in dynamic ways, and the lungs were crafted to breathe. The mind was created to think, reason, focus, and manifest in wild creativity. The human heart was made to feel profound love and joy, anger, grief, and despair. The fact that we now live in a world where practices like conscious movement, mindful breathing, and meditation seem odd and out of place has more to do with a world out of balance than it has to with the practice of yoga. The miracle of yoga is not that it enables us to do supernatural things, but rather to do that which is in our very nature.

70

Every action, whether noble or immoral, is preceded by thought. That thought may be conscious or unconscious, ignorant or mindful. The only way to act from a posture of loving kindness and compassion is to heal the mind. That is why we meditate.

71

To witness your life—the highs and lows,
the times of chaos, and the periods
of order—without trying to control or
manipulate—is the key to inner calm. This
nonjudgmental observation of the world
allows us to let go of condition-based
happiness and embrace true contentment.

72

Forgiveness is not something we do; rather
it is a process of reminding yourself over and
over again that holding a resentment only
hurts yourself. Once you embrace that truth
fully, forgiveness simply happens on its own.

73

All suffering in this world is a result of
someone, somewhere, not living his or her
life's purpose. Through spiritual practice,
your life's purpose is revealed. Through
spiritual practice, the courage to live your
life's purpose is developed. Through spiritual
practice, suffering is eased—your own
suffering and the suffering of the world.

74

Time is an illusion created by the ego for the
sole purpose of denying the unbreakable bond
between cause and effect. Mindfulness joins
the mind with the present moment, where
the illusion of time dissolves without effort,
where cause and effect are correctly seen as
unbroken, unbreakable, and inseparable.

75

Duality—dark and light, good and evil, high and low—defines more than just the external world. It is the essence of the body, heart, and mind as well. To be at peace with the duality of the world, we first need to be at peace with the ebb and flow of our own emotional, mental, and physical tides.

76

At the root of all suffering, whether personal
or societal, is the false perception of
separation. Yoga, in all it forms, is the practice
of healing the mind by joining together
that which is perceived to be separate.

77

Rather than sacrificing logic and critical thought, yoga invites us to more fully use our ability to think and reason.

Rather than asking us to deny our emotions—the light and the dark—yoga teaches us to embrace what we feel.

Rather than denying the body's appetites and impulses, yoga reminds us to trust our instincts more fully.

78

A prison cell, however tastefully decorated,
is still a cage.

79

Like other animals, humans have the inherent ability to heal and find balance. We don't need books, or teachers, or fancy diets. The answers we seek are encoded in our cells. While we have this innate ability to heal, purification is usually a prerequisite . That is why we do hatha yoga.

A mud pie is, at the end of the day, attractively packaged mud. A life spent in pursuit of comfort and leisure — of being a slave to your attachments — is, at the end of the day, attractively packaged suffering.

81

Each time we come to savasana, we practice dying—we surrender the body to the earth and prepare for our destiny in this life. Facing death and embracing mortality is the key to living. We may fear it, resist it, and spend untold hours dreading it, But our mortality is the place where our human nature comes face to face with our divine nature. In a very real sense, death is our greatest teacher and the one true guru.

82

Praying for peace is wonderful; meditations on loving kindness and compassion are sublime; acts of generosity and healing have the power to change the world. But when all three come together in a selfless act of devotion, miracles occur.

83

The problem is not the unhappiness and disappointment you feel at harvest time; the problem is the seeds you planted last spring.

84

Within each being exists the voice of wisdom:
a quiet and unassuming voice that longs to
guide us out of darkness, to lift the veil of
ignorance and shepherd the seeker to higher
ground. Whether one calls it the Sadguru, the
Holy Spirit, or the Still Small Voice, one thing
is certain—this inner voice will never yell or
compete for attention. Only by quieting the
mind can this voice be heard. But when you
take the time to listen—really listen—this voice
is as evident as the warm sun on your face.

85

Spiritual practice lives at the corner of
self-respect and self-discipline.

86

This life is a dream—sometimes a dream of beauty— sometimes a terrifying nightmare. We will all wake from this dream eventually. Spiritual practice allows us first to transform the dream from one of terror to one of joy, and then from a dream of joy, to awakening to our true nature as Atman.

87

Procrastination is the enemy of
accomplishment—not simply because the
task you are avoiding fails to get done, but
because all of your other goals and objectives
get mired in the same sandpit as well.

88

My mind has evolved from that of a child to that of an adult and passed through countless changes along the way. My heart has known great love, heartache, joy, and anger—it has shifted directions more often than the wind. My body began as two cells, has grown, aged, and passed through sickness and health. Even the face in my mirror is far different than the one that once stared back at me just a few months ago. But through this state of flux that has defined my life, there is a part of me that has been entirely the same throughout. This changeless part of me has sat quietly witnessing, at peace and smiling softly.

89

The only place healing can occur,
wisdom can be realized, compassion
can be extended, and peace can be
experienced, is the present moment.

Yoga can give you greater health and longevity, but these benefits can also become distractions from the greater truth that yoga seeks to reveal. Even the most disciplined yogis will sometimes fall ill, and longevity is never eternal. Yoga's true gift is the recognition that while health and longevity may be nice, peace and joy are not dependent on these temporary conditions. Once a yogi recognizes this, the true journey begins. Living to avoid pain, sickness, and death is not living at all. It is like removing a bandage one hair at a time.

91

Yoga gives you the freedom to choose, but it does not guarantee you will choose freedom.

92

Yoga and meditation not only give us the
ability to enjoy the beautiful moments in
life, but also the ability to fully embrace the
difficult and ugly moments. So often we
define success in our practice by the way
we feel in a given moment, but practice
is never about select peak moments.
Practice is about celebrating the fullness of
life—the difficult and the easy, the beautiful
and the ugly, the savory and the sweet.

93

The ego mind is like a plant growing in
a very small pot. While the pot may be
attractive and ornate, its size doesn't allow
the plant to express its full potential.

94

Given the choice, most children would have ice cream for dinner. Similarly, yogis prefer the highs of yoga, the so-called "good practice." But just as healthy children require vegetables and whole grains, advanced yogis need to be challenged during practice. The peak experiences we have during practice may keep us coming back to the mat, but it is the difficult and unpleasant aspects of practice that make us strong and prepare us for the challenges of life.

95

The needle on your moral compass is made
of compassion. Without compassion you may
have a moral compass, but you only have
a one in four chance of finding true north.

96

The mantra of the victim is, "If not for the
events and circumstances of the world, I
would be happy." The world is often unfair
and unjust, but that alone is not enough to
create a victim. Victims believe they lack the
power to choose. While you may not always
be able to choose the circumstances of
your life, you can choose how you respond.
Through spiritual practice, we can choose
inner harmony even when the world around
us is filled with pain, suffering, and chaos.

97

You may think you see the world clearly—that the people in your life and even those you have never met are easily understood—that the things that fill your home, your community, and the world are benign and neutral. But every thing your eyes rest upon, every sound your ears hear, every thought and memory that passes through your awareness is filtered through the distorted lens of your perception. In reality, the people and things that fill your life have only the meaning that you have projected onto them. When we meditate, we pause the perception projector--however briefly—and we see the world a bit more clearly. It is in this clarity that we find wisdom, compassion, and true healing.

98

The miracle of yoga is not that we get to
reshape the external world—to bend the
laws of time and space. The miracle of yoga
is that we get to reshape our perception
of the external world. Where we once only
perceived injuries, illness, and pain, we now
see an opportunity for growth. Where we
once perceived acrimony and discord in
relationships, we are now able to experience
deep empathy. Where we once perceived
darkness, evil, injustice, and vexing social
issues, we now perceive the opportunity to
serve. Yoga is like a purifying fire that burns
away false perceptions of the world and
of ourselves to enable us to see clearly.

What defines you? Is it those hazy memories
of yesterday, or last year, or childhood?
Is it the emotions and thoughts that are
passing through you in this very moment?
Is it the future where you achieve or even
fail to achieve the goals you set? Or are you
defined by something bigger than all that?
Something that is beyond the change, beyond
the fluctuations of your life? To practice
mindfulness is to see that it is your changeless
nature that truly defines you, rather than the
ebb and flow of your emotional tides or the
shifting directions of your thought streams.

100

Pain is powerful medicine. While it may be unpleasant to take this medicine, it is what shapes and inspires us. As you review the story of your life, you will find that growth was almost always preceded by hardship—the loss of a job, the passing of a loved one, challenges with health, the end of a relationship. Rather than avoiding pain, yoga asks us to surrender to it, to look deep into it, and to be healed by it.

101

The good news is that attachment is not an industrial strength glue that binds the mind to condition-based happiness. You can free your mind at any moment by simply letting go—simply relax the mind the way you would unclench your fist.

102

An advanced yoga practice has less to do
with what happens when you roll out your
mat and move through your practice and
more to do with what happens when you
roll up your mat and move through life.

103

Injuries happen on the yoga mat all the time, but they never happen when we are truly practicing yoga. For instance, most yoga-related neck injuries happen when you strain yourself trying to see what is happening on the yoga mat next to yours.

104

Most yoga practice starts with the goal of
doing the extraordinary and supernatural—
to place the feet behind the head, balance
on one hand, or cheat the aging process.
But the true practice of yoga aims at doing
the natural and the ordinary—to stand
on your feet, to find joy in filling the lungs,
and to release with each exhalation.

105

Contrary to popular belief, the translation of
vinyasa is not "sweaty practice." Vinyasa is
connecting breath and movement—a practice
that has nothing to do with moving fast,
accelerating the heart rate, or manifesting
a pool of sweat. It does, however, have
everything to do with mindful movement.

106

Relationship with another is like gazing
into a still pond. You will either see your
own face reflected or the depth of the
water, but never both at the same time.

107

A gardener cannot make a seed grow.
She can simply create the conditions for
growth to occur and then patiently wait.

A physician cannot heal the body. She
can simply create the conditions for
healing to occur and then patiently wait.

A spiritual seeker cannot enlighten the
mind or fill the heart with compassion.
She can simply create the conditions for
grace to pour in and then patiently wait.

108

If you live well, you will be shocked and surprised to see how, at the end of your life, it all turns out. But like any great novel, the clues have always been there and the plot twists and turns were hidden in plain sight.

Acknowledgements

Special thanks to my family:

My son Jaden Patrick Main

My mother Kathy Ascare

My father John Main

My brother Jason Main and my sister Jennifer Holdridge

My nieces Zoe Main, Haley Holdridge and Lauren and Emma Glaza and my nephews, Wyatt Holdridge Chase, Jake and Tyler Flynn

Don, Amy, Alden, Josie, Joe, John, Sarah, Peter, Linda, Kate, Gus, Adelina, Arthur and Mary, and all the other Mains who are too numerous to mention.

Special thanks to the many friends who have supported me so much:

Wanda Pierce, Lance King, Ellie Brown-Gee, Jim Healey, Rose Sattler, Michael Lynch, Christopher Love, Jasper Trout, Michael Watson, Danni Pomplun, Dustin Finkle, Joel Klausler, Heather Peterson, Blake Tucker, Seth Ellis, Jack Mueller, Alexander Smith, Tim Dale, Tara Dale, Sean Haleen,

To the clergy, staff and volunteers at Grace Cathedral:

Bishop Marc Andrus, The Very Rev. Dr. Malcolm Clemens Young, The Rev. Jude Harmon, The Rev. Beth Grundy, Katherine Thompson. To all the musicians, support team, Board of Trustees, and most especially the students!

To my editors:

Sue Louiseau, Peter Wong, Michelle Dickson and Andrea Drugan,Dave Evans, Stephanie Sandberg, Constance Cummings, Linda Raj, Kevin Fisher-Paulson, Holly Heffelbower, Justine T. Fan

Vivien Wang, Jeff Coffing and Ericka Montana, ERYT

Special thanks to Michael Fantasia for designing this book, and to Ryan Scott for the author photo.

49271747R00076

Made in the USA
Lexington, KY
30 January 2016